WILDFLOWERS

of the Desert Southwest

MEG QUINN

Rio Nuevo Publishers
Tucson, Arizona

Rio Nuevo Publishers
An imprint of Treasure Chest Books
P.O. Box 5250
Tucson, AZ 85703-0250

© 2000 Meg Quinn
All Rights Reserved

ISBN 1-887896-25-2

Editor: Ronald J. Foreman
Designer: William Benoit, Simpson & Convent
Photos © David Bertelsen except:
© Jim Honcoop, 11, 13, 18 (bottom), 19, 20, 25,
    26, 27, 31, 33, 51, 61, 67, 68, 74, 76, 78
© George H.H. Huey, cover
© Meg Quinn, 22, 30, 39, 41, 55, 65
© Antoinette Segade, 41, 47
© Jon Mark Stewart, 1, 5, 12, 14, 16, 28, 36, 38
    (both), 40, 46, 52, 53, 63, 77, 81, 83

Printed in Korea
10 9 8 7 6 5 4 3 2 1

INTRODUCTION

I t is a rare and unforgettable experience to see the Southwest deserts blanketed with spring wildflowers in a banner year. Only once a decade or so, optimal conditions can lead to a truly glorious display.

Tourists from across the nation and around the world flock to desert wildflower "hot spots" to enjoy the spectacle. They wander through shimmering fields of goldpoppy, lupine, and owl clover— cameras clicking to capture what is surely a miraculous event. Local residents likewise are filled with wonder to see their desert home, typically a place of subtle color, carpeted with rich hues of gold, azure, magenta, pink, and purple.

Flowers that produce the most glorious and abundant color in Southwest deserts are the spring annuals. These plants live only for a brief period and must complete their life cycle relatively quickly. They are examples of what ecologists call "drought escapers," which means they avoid extreme heat and aridity by simply existing as seed until conditions are favorable. Seeds of many desert annuals can remain viable for a decade or more. Many species have chemical inhibitors on the seed that will prevent germination except under ideal conditions. An inch or so of rain in the fall of the year, coupled with mild soil temperatures, generally will trigger mass germination. These conditions also provide the most likely environment for a seedling to complete its life cycle.

It is crucial that these short-lived plants are able to flower and produce seed to insure the survival of the species. In some years, good fall rain will be followed by a prolonged drought. In this scenario, the plants often will manage to flower and set seed, but in a severely stunted form. For a really sensational year to occur, a good fall rain must be followed by consistent monthly rains throughout the winter and early spring.

Even in an average year, a surprising number of annual species can be found, although not necessarily in expansive "carpets." Wildflower enthusiasts may need to seek out canyon trails or other sheltered environments to find the elusive survivors. Along with the spectacular annuals, many desert perennials will come into bloom during this same period, producing equally stunning bursts of color. These showy perennials—including brittlebush (*Encelia farinosa*), desert marigold (*Baileya multiradiata*), and Parry penstemon (*Penstemon parryi*)—do not have such specific requirements in order to bloom. Many desert perennials will flower in response to rain at almost any time during the year.

NORTH AMERICAN DESERTS

Deserts are not so easy to define yet they share certain common characteristics. Most importantly, deserts exhibit low precipitation, high daytime temperatures, and frequent wind. Evaporation from the soil and from plants exceeds precipitation, resulting in periodic drought. Also, rainfall in deserts is highly variable and unpredictable. The four major deserts of North America each have distinctive rainfall regimes, temperature extremes, soils, and characteristic vegetation.

The Great Basin Desert is the northernmost and highest in elevation, with very cold winters. Annual precipitation ranges from six to twelve inches, and most of it falls in winter as snow. Winter lows often are below freezing and summer highs frequently exceed one hundred degrees Fahrenheit. The topography ranges from 2,000 to 5,000 feet, and low, rounded shrubs dominate the landscape. The most common is big sagebrush (*Artemesia tridentata*), which often grows in nearly

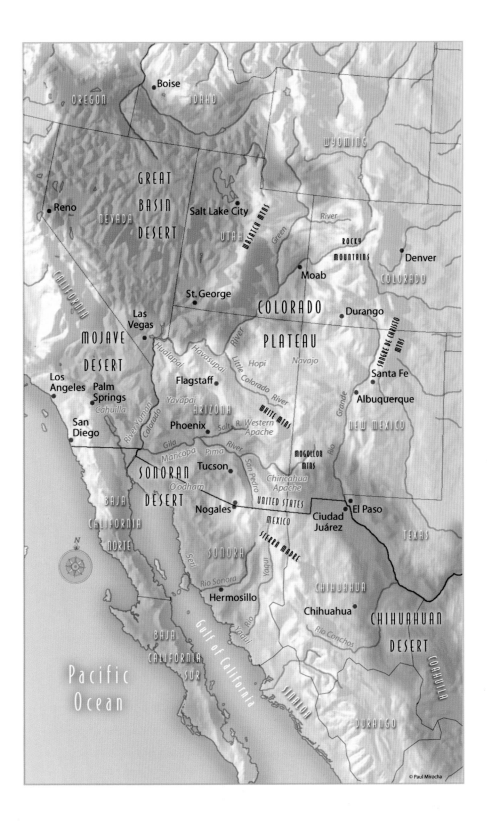

OREGON

Boise

IDAHO

WYOMING

GREAT

BASIN

Reno

NEVADA

DESERT

Salt Lake City

UTAH

WASATCH MTNS

Green

River

ROCKY

MOUNTAINS

Denver

COLORADO

Moab

St. George

COLORADO

Durango

Las
Vegas

PLATEAU

SANGRE DE CRISTO MTNS

MOJAVE

Hualapai

Havasupai

River

Hopi

Navajo

Santa Fe

DESERT

Little Colorado River

Flagstaff

Los
Angeles

Palm
Springs

Yavapai

Albuquerque

Cahuilla

ARIZONA

WHITE MTNS

San
Diego

River Yuman

Colorado

Phoenix

Salt

R. Western

Grande

NEW MEXICO

Gila

Apache

Maricopa

Pima

River

SONORAN

Tucson

San Pedro

MOGOLLON
MTNS

Rio

O'odham

Chiricahua
Apache

DESERT

Nogales

UNITED STATES

El Paso

BAJA

MEXICO

Ciudad
Juárez

CALIFORNIA

Seri

SONORA

NORTE

SIERRA MADRE

TEXAS

Yaqui

N

CHIHUAHUA

Rio Sonora

Hermosillo

Chihuahua

CHIHUAHUAN

Rio

Baja

Yaqui

Rio Conchos

DESERT

CALIFORNIA

COAHUILA

SUR

Pacific
Ocean

Gulf of California

SINALOA

DURANGO

© Paul Mirocha

pure stands. Annuals and herbaceous perennials are less abundant than in other North American deserts.

The Mojave Desert is the driest and the smallest of the deserts, with an average annual rainfall of two to five inches, which falls mainly in winter and spring. Winters are cold and hard freezes are common. Vegetation consists mainly of low shrubs, including creosote bush (*Larrea tridentata*) and white bursage (*Ambrosia dumosa*). Prickly pear and cholla (*Opuntia* species) are the most abundant types of cacti. The arborescent yucca known as Joshua tree (*Yucca brevifolia*) dominates the landscape at elevations above 3,000 feet and roughly delineates the boundaries of the Mojave Desert. In response to winter storms, many species of spring annuals are evident in a good year.

A bi-seasonal rainfall pattern and mild winters characterize the Sonoran Desert, which features an impressive variety of life forms. These include columnar cacti such as saguaro (*Carnegiea gigantea*),

legume trees, numerous types of smaller cacti, leaf succulents, shrubs, perennials, and annual wildflowers. Gentle winter rains sweep into the region from the Pacific Ocean, while summer thunderstorms originate in the gulfs of Mexico and California. The Sonoran is a low, hot, subtropical desert that ranges in elevation from below sea level to 3,500 feet and covers about one hundred thousand square miles.

The Chihuahuan Desert ranges in elevation from 1,000 to 6,500 feet. Vegetation is mainly a variety of small shrubs, leaf succulents, and numerous species of small cacti. Lechuguilla (*Agave lechuguilla*) is a major dominant in a large portion of this desert. Rainfall averages about six to fifteen inches annually, occurs primarily in summer, and originates in the Gulf of Mexico. Some winter rain falls in the northernmost regions, which results in occasional spectacular blooms of spring annuals. Hard winter freezes are common.

ABOUT THIS BOOK

Some field guides include annuals, perennials, shrubs, trees, and cacti in their definition of "wildflower." This guide uses a somewhat narrower definition and aims to show primarily the annuals, herbaceous perennials, and a few woody shrubs. The regional focus is mainly the Sonoran and Mojave deserts, although many of these plants range into the Great Basin and Chihuahuan deserts as well. In most cases, the maximum size of the plant has been given. Size will vary considerably depending on factors such as temperature, soil moisture, and geographic location. Flowering times may also vary with location and environmental conditions. Please consult the glossary for definitions of technical terms encountered in the text.

Since numerous plants depicted here are in the sunflower family (*Asteraceae*), a diagram of a common sunflower has been included (right), along with a drawing of a more "typical" type of flower (left).

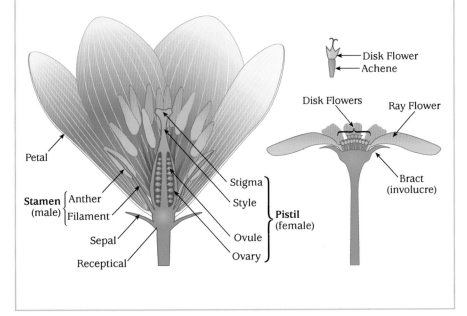

CONSERVATION

Destruction of habitat and loss of biological diversity in the Southwest deserts is as serious a concern as it is in other parts of the country and, indeed, the world. Many types of human influences have had a detrimental impact on our fragile desert ecosystems. These range from inappropriate livestock grazing and off-road vehicle recreation to urban sprawl, mining, and agriculture.

One of the single greatest threats today is the invasion of exotic weeds. Some of the most serious and widespread invaders are buffelgrass, Mediterranean grass, annual brome grasses, filaree, and certain mustards. These alien invaders often colonize areas so aggressively  that they displace native species, particularly annuals. Should this trend continue, it could pose a serious threat to the spectacular spring wildflower displays we so anticipate. Many of these weeds, particularly the grasses, also create a fire hazard. Most desert shrubs and trees are not fire adapted and will not recover from severe wildfires.

Only through the combined efforts of concerned public and private organizations and committed individuals will we be able to effectively control and manage the spread of exotic species and other threats to desert environments. We hope that field guides such as this one will stimulate a greater interest in, and appreciation for, the native flora and, in turn, the desire to preserve it.

Sand Verbena
Abronia villosa

Family
Four O'Clock–Nyctaginaceae

C ommonly associated with dunes, beaches, and dry streambeds,
sand verbena has prostrate, sticky stems that clamber freely
over sandy soils. Showy clusters of fragrant, deep pink to purple,
tubular blossoms are attractive to butterflies and moths. Individual
blossoms are about one inch long. Succulent, oval shaped leaves
are deep green, with fine hairs. Sand verbena is an annual that
often produces striking
spring displays on otherwise
barren sandy habitats. Sand
verbena is not a true verbena,
but is a member of the four
o'clock family.

Elevation: Below 1,500 feet

Range: Sandy habitats of the
Mojave and Sonoran deserts

Trailing Four O'Clock (Windmills)
Allionia incarnata

Family
Four O'Clock–Nyctaginaceae

A ground-hugging, vining perennial, trailing four o'clock is a common roadside plant with deep pink, sometimes pale or white, one-inch diameter flowers. The "flower" is actually a cluster of three or four flowers that grow together and bloom simultaneously. You can gently tug on the sepals to see the developing ovary, or fruit, at the base of each flower. Butterflies and bees visit the flowers to feed on nectar. Leaves are up to two inches long, oval, with pointed tips and prominent veins. Trailing four o'clock is common in disturbed areas, on rocky slopes, and along washes. It blooms intermittently from spring through fall. An infusion of the root has been used by the Navajo to treat swellings. The Seri made a tea of the leaves as a cure for diarrhea.

Elevation: Below 6,000 feet

Range: All North American deserts and south into South America

Fairy Duster (False Mesquite)
Calliandra eriophylla

Family
Legume–Fabaceae

Fairy duster is a compact, woody shrub that grows up to three feet tall and has small, pinnately compound leaves. A mass of blooms covers the plant in late winter and intermittently in summer in response to rain. Flower color ranges from white to a brilliant rose pink, though pale pink blooms are most common. The blossoms are mostly comprised of stamen clusters with highly reduced petals, and are visited by numerous bees, butterflies, and insects. The fruit is a two-inch flat pod, edged with a prominent ridge. Upon maturity, the pods will snap open, flinging the seed far from the mother plant. Curled remnants of the pods will often remain attached to the plant for several weeks or months.

Elevation: Below 5,000 feet

Range: Sonoran Desert

New Mexico Thistle (Desert Thistle)
Circium neomexicanum

Family
Sunflower–Asteraceae

Sometimes growing to a height of six feet or more, New Mexico thistle is a robust biennial or perennial that is covered with prickly foliage and bears dense clusters of showy, pinkish-lilac flowers. Flower heads are typically about three inches wide. Numerous butterflies, bees, and insects are attracted to the flowers and serve as pollinators.

Leaves are up ten inches long, with woolly hairs and sharp, spiny teeth along the margins. Lesser goldfinches often devour the seeds of New Mexico thistles. Some birds also use the downy hairs of the seeds for nesting material. The Navajo used the plant in a treatment for chills and fever, and as an eye wash.

Elevation: 1,000–6,500 feet

Range: Mojave, Sonoran, and Great Basin deserts

Desert Five-spot
Eremalche rotundifolia

Family
Mallow–Malvaceae

A n unusual, attractive annual that is most common in the Mojave desert, desert five-spot bears partially open, globe-shaped, bright pink or lilac flowers and has broad, toothed, heart-shaped leaves. Peering into the flower, you'll notice a large, dark red, fringed spot at the base of each petal. These ornate spots actually serve as directional signals for nectar-seeking bees. The fruit is a flat disk with several one-seeded segments. Desert five-spot grows one to two feet tall, and is found on open, gravelly plains and in sandy washes, blooming from March through May. Flowers open in the afternoon and appear translucent when light passes through.

Elevation: 100–1,500 feet

Range: Mojave and western Sonoran deserts

Parry Penstemon

Penstemon parryi

Family
Figwort–Scrophulariaceae

Common in desert washes, Parry penstemon is an extremely showy perennial, with clusters of brilliant pink, tubular blossoms occurring along a flower spike up to four feet in height. Penstemons are often called "beardtongue" due to the sterile, usually bearded or brush-tipped stamen, that lies within the lower part of the corolla. Flowers of Parry penstemon are about three quarters of an inch long and funnel shaped, with rounded petal lobes. They are pollinated primarily by hummingbirds, but are also visited by moths, bees, and other insects. Carpenter bees frequently can be seen raiding nectar from the base of the flowers. In the first year of growth, a basal rosette of bluish green, lance-shaped leaves will develop. The following year, the tall flower spike will emerge. Many species of penstemon are easily cultivated in Southwest gardens. Plants can be obtained in nurseries or germinated from seed in fall or winter.

Elevation: 1,000–5,000 feet

Range: Sonoran Desert

Mojave Beardtongue
(Desert Penstemon)
Penstemon pseudospectabilis

Family
Figwort–Scrophulariaceae

Mojave beardtongue produces a striking floral display. The pale pink to deep rose flowers occur along numerous stalks, up to four feet in height. Corollas are slightly inflated, and up to one inch in length. The sterile stamen is not bearded. Fruits are upright, conical capsules that split open at the tip when mature and release several small, black seeds. Leaves are gray-green, prominently toothed, and fused around the flowering stem. Mojave beardtongue blooms from February to May.

Elevation: 2,000–7,000 feet

Range: Mojave and Sonoran deserts

Wire Lettuce (Desert Straw)
Stephanomeria pauciflora

Family
Sunflower–Asteraceae

Wire lettuce is easily overlooked except when in bloom, due to the bare, often dead-looking stems and sparse foliage. The three-quarter-inch, lavender heads consist solely of ray flowers and can bloom almost any time of the year in response to rain. Brownish, feathery bristles are attached to the achenes and help carry them on the wind. Wire lettuce is found in washes, and on slopes and sandy plains. Hopi women have used the root of wire lettuce to increase a mother's milk supply.

Elevation: Below 7,000 feet

Range: Chihuahuan, Mojave, and Sonoran deserts

Wild Onion (Desert Onion)
Allium macropetalum

Family
Lily–Liliaceae

lusters of delicate white to pale pink flowers appear on the narrow stem tips of wild onion in early spring. Individual flowers are about one half inch long, with the midrib of each petal striped with pink. The grassy, succulent leaves and underground bulbs smell and taste similar to the familiar cultivated onion. Wild onion blooms March to June on rocky slopes and gravelly bajadas. The Navajo and other tribes ate the one-inch bulbs raw, or by first rubbing them in hot ashes to remove the strong taste. Cooked bulbs were often dried and stored for later use.

Elevation: 1,000–7,000 feet

Range: Great Basin, Sonoran, and Chihuahuan deserts

Desert Anemone (Windflower)

Anemone tuberosa

Family
Crowfoot–Ranunculaceae

Desert anemone is an early spring perennial growing to one and a half feet in height and flowering in late February and early March. Flowers are showy and up to one and a half inches wide. The white to pale pink "petals" are actually sepals that fall away, leaving the cylindrical seed head. This head ultimately disintegrates, dropping the seed to the ground. Leaves are mostly basal and highly divided. Desert anemone is typically found on rocky desert slopes and in canyons. As a member of the Crowfoot family, anemone is related to larkspur and columbine.

Elevation: 2,500–5,000 feet

Range: Great Basin, Sonoran, and Chihuahuan deserts

Prickly Poppy (Cowboy's Fried Egg)
Argemone pleiacantha

Family

Poppy–Papaveraceae

Prickly poppy is a tall and unmistakable perennial wildflower. Stems can grow to four feet with flowers up to five inches across. White crinkled petals resembling crepe paper surround a large cluster of bright yellow stamens. Bluish green foliage, stems, and buds are covered with thorny prickles. Prickly poppy will bloom in spring, summer, and fall as long as conditions are favorable. Mourning doves feed on the seeds that are found inside the prickly capsules. The plant is poisonous to livestock and can be an indicator of overgrazed grassland. Prickly poppy is common in disturbed areas, on roadsides, and in washes. Though it has been used medicinally, the plant contains numerous alkaloids and can be highly toxic. A tea of the leaves has been used by the Seri to treat kidney pain, as a diuretic, and as a postpartum medicine. The Pima boiled the leaves to wash wounds.

Elevation: 1,500–8,000 feet

Range: Great Basin and Sonoran deserts

Desert Milkweed
(Leafless Milkweed)
Asclepias subulata

Family

Milkweed–Asclepidaceae

Desert milkweed, a perennial growing to four feet, remains leafless for much of the year, and only produces leaves briefly in response to summer rains. The erect, gray-green stems contain a milky sap that can be poisonous to livestock and humans. White to pale yellow flower clusters appear in spring and continue to bloom intermittently throughout the summer. Milkweed flowers have an inner ring of upright "hoods," and an outer ring of petals. Pollen is contained in pollinia—paired structures that hook onto the legs of visiting insects. The tarantula hawk (actually a large wasp) and other insects feed on the nectar-rich flowers, and serve as pollinators. Milkweed fruits are the classic inflated pod, bursting at maturity and releasing round, flat seeds that are carried on the wind by the long, silky hairs. Desert milkweed and other milkweeds are important larval food plants for the queen and monarch butterflies. The poisonous sap makes them toxic to predators, both as caterpillars and adult butterflies. Desert butterfly gardens often include milkweeds to encourage the *en masse* presence of these creatures. The Pima used desert milkweed to induce vomiting and as an eye medicine.

Elevation: Below 3,000 feet

Range: Sonoran Desert

White Tackstem
Calycoseris wrightii

Family
Sunflower–Asteraceae

White tackstem is an annual with milky sap that grows up to fifteen inches in height. Flower heads are showy, one to two inches across, and occur at the stem tips. The creamy white to pale yellow ray flowers range between fifteen and twenty-five per head and are tinged with purple underneath. Leaves are bluish green, basal, and highly divided into thin, linear lobes. Glands on the stems that resemble tacks distinguish white tackstem from desert chicory. Desert chicory is also a larger plant with fewer ray flowers. White tackstem blooms from March to May on open gravelly plains, in washes, and on dry hillsides.

Elevation: 500–4,000 feet

Range: Mojave, Sonoran, and Chihuahuan deserts

Brown-eyed Primrose

Camissonia claviformis *var.* aurantiaca

Family
Evening Primrose–Onagraceae

Brown-eyed primrose is a common spring annual that grows up to twelve inches high, with pendulous buds, and clusters of white flowers that bear a conspicuous brownish red center. The fruits are erect, club-shaped pods. Brown-eyed primrose and other species of *Camissonia* are important larval food plants and nectar sources for the white line sphinx moth. The caterpillars feed on the leaves and the adults feed on nectar from the night-blooming flowers. A type of native bee serves as the primary pollinator. Brown-eyed primrose prefers sandy or gravelly soils.

Elevation: Below 4,500 feet

Range: Mojave, Sonoran, and Great Basin deserts

Morning Bride (Desert Pincushion)
Chaenactis fremontii

Family
Sunflower–Asteraceae

A common spring annual, morning bride grows as tall as sixteen inches and produces white or pinkish disk flowers in pincushion-like heads. Heads are about one inch in width. The leaves are divided into slender, linear lobes, and usually are clustered at the base of the plant. Morning bride can be found blooming from March to June in sandy or gravelly habitats, often under creosote and other desert shrubs.

Elevation:
1,000–3,500 feet

Range: Mojave and Sonoran deserts

Popcorn Flower
Cryptantha angustifolia

Family
Borage–Boraginaceae

Popcorn flower is an extremely common spring annual that grows from just a few inches to one and one half feet in height. The miniature, white, tubular flowers are arranged in a coiled, scorpion-like cluster. Most insects cannot get to the pollen inside the tiny opening in the flowers. One type of small, solitary bee, however, is able to remove the pollen without entering the flower. The stems and foliage are densely covered with stiff, white, bristly hairs. Popcorn flower is common on gravelly plains and in sandy washes, blooming from February to June. There are many species of *Cryptantha* and they can be difficult to distinguish without the aid of a floral key and a microscope.

Elevation: Below 4,000 feet

Range: Mojave, Sonoran, and Chihuahuan deserts

Sacred Datura (Jimson Weed)
Datura wrightii

Family

Nightshade–Solanaceae

A sprawling, large-leaved perennial, sacred datura produces striking, large, trumpet-shaped flowers that open in the early evening and are pollinated by hawkmoths. The corollas are up to ten inches long and tinged with purple, and their sweet fragrance serves to attract the moths. Leaves are up to six inches long, oval to heart-shaped, with prominent veins. The fruit is a prickly capsule that breaks apart at maturity. All parts of the plant, including the nectar, are extremely poisonous. Ingestion can cause fever, delirium, convulsions, and death.

In spite of these dangers, sacred datura has been one of the most universally used hallucinogenic and medicinal plants in the Southwest. The Pima used the nectar from the flower buds in a treatment for sore eyes. Hopi medicine men chewed the roots to induce visions while making a diagnosis. The Seri brewed tea from the seeds to relieve sore throat, and made a poultice of the leaves to treat boils. Cahuilla shamans ingested sacred datura to transcend reality, and to contact specific guardian spirits.

Elevation: 1,000–6,000 feet

Range: All North American deserts

Fleabane Daisy

Erigeron divergens

Family
Sunflower–Asteraceae

Fleabane daisy is an annual or perennial spring wildflower with a broad elevational range. The flower heads are about an inch in diameter and are clustered at stem tips, with white, narrow rays and bright yellow disk flowers. The rays are often tinged with lavender, particularly on the underside. Stems are weak and spreading, branching from the base to about twenty inches tall. Leaves are narrow, linear, and covered with soft hairs. Fleabane daisy prefers sandy or gravelly soils and spreads easily, forming large patches in the landscape.

Elevation: 1,000–9,000 feet

Range: All North American deserts

Woolly Daisy
Eriophyllum lanosum

Family
Sunflower–Asteraceae

Woolly daisy is a petite annual that grows only a few inches high. Flower heads are about a half inch across with white or rosy rays and yellow centers. Leaves are silvery gray and are covered with soft, woolly hairs. Woolly daisy blooms from February to May, and is typically found on dry, gravelly flats and hillsides, often under shrubs.

Elevation: 1,000–3,000 feet

Range: Mojave and Sonoran deserts

Desert Lily (Ajo Lily)
Hesperocallis undulata

Family
Lily–Liliaceae

Desert Lily is a spectacular perennial that emerges from a two-inch diameter bulb that can be as deep as two feet underground. The large, Easter lily-like flowers occur along an unbranched stem that can grow to three feet high under favorable conditions. Individual flowers are two to three inches long and funnel shaped, with green stripes along the mid-vein of each petal. The long, wavy-edged basal leaves can reach a length of twenty inches. Flowers open at night and are sweetly scented and attractive to the hawkmoth, the primary pollinator. Desert lily is found almost exclusively on sandy flats and dune areas and blooms from February to April. The underground bulbs were baked or eaten raw by the Tohono O'odham, Pima, Yuma, and Cahuilla.

Elevation: Below 2,000 feet

Range: Mojave and Sonoran deserts

Pepper Grass
Lepidium virginicum *var.* medium

Family
Mustard–Brassicaceae

One of many spring-blooming, annual mustards, peppergrass has a hot, pungent flavor, hence its name. Delicate, white flowers form clusters around the stem tips. The plant itself can grow to a height of about two feet, with multiple branches. Blooms can be found as early as December and as late as May. The abundant, round, flat, two-seeded fruits may persist on the plant for several weeks. Peppergrass is very common on rocky slopes, gravelly flats, disturbed soils, and in washes. The Tohono O'odham ate the seeds and parched, dried, and stored them for future use. The Seri ate the whole plant, fresh or dried, and also used it to flavor meat.

Elevation: Below 5,000 feet

Range: All North American deserts

Blackfoot Daisy

Melampodium leucanthum

Family
Sunflower–Asteraceae

Blackfoot daisy is a showy perennial that forms a low mound and branches freely from the base of the plant. The flower heads are about one and one half inches across, with white rays that surround a cluster of yellow disk flowers. Leaves are dark green, narrow, and up to two inches long. Blackfoot daisy prefers limestone soils and occurs on dry, rocky slopes, grasslands, and oak woodlands. It is a popular groundcover in Southwest gardens.

Elevation: 2,000–5,000 feet

Range: Chihuahuan and Sonoran deserts

Four O'Clock
(Wishbone Four O'Clock)
Mirabilis bigelovii

Family
Four O'Clock–Nyctaginaceae

F our o'clock flowers bloom in the late afternoon and remain open into the following morning. The delicate flowers are white and up to three quarters of an inch wide. Leaves are dark green, oval to round. A weak-stemmed perennial with sticky stems, four o'clock is found on rocky slopes, in canyons, and on desert grasslands. Branching stems form a wishbone pattern. Four o'clock can bloom as early as February and as late as November, in response to rain.

Elevation: Below 4,700 feet

Range: Mojave and Sonoran deserts

Desert Star
Monoptilon bellioides

Family
Sunflower–Asteraceae

D esert Star is a prostrate annual that grows only one to three inches high but spreads up to ten inches wide under favorable conditions. The striking, relatively large flower heads often dwarf the plant itself. Rays are snow-white to rosy, drying to a bluish color. Reddish stems branch and spread from the base. The leaves are covered with stiff hairs. Desert Star blooms from February to April on sandy or rocky slopes, mesas, and desert flats.

Elevation: 200–3,500 feet

Range: Mojave and Sonoran deserts

Desert Tobacco
Nicotiana obtusifolia (trigonophylla)

Family
Nightshade–Solanaceae

An annual or perennial growing to three feet in height, desert tobacco bears cream to greenish white, tubular blossoms with flared petal lobes. The sticky, oval or lance-shaped leaves are foul smelling and contain nicotine. Desert tobacco is commonly found in washes and on rocky slopes, and blooms intermittently throughout the year in response to rain. Leaves of desert tobacco were smoked in ceremonies by the Hopi and Cahuilla, and also smoked casually by the Tohono O'odham, Pima, and Havasupai. The Cahuilla used the leaves to treat wounds and ear infections. The related tree tobacco (*Nicotiana glauca*) has yellow flowers and is a South American native that has naturalized throughout the Southwest.

Elevation: Below 6,000 feet

Range: All North American deserts

Dune Primrose (Bird Cage Primrose)
Oenothera deltoides

Family
Evening Primrose–Onagraceae

Dune primrose is a spring blooming annual that can grow to a foot in height. Individual flowers are large, up to three and a half inches across, and pure white with yellow centers. The prominent, cross-shaped stigma is characteristic of the genus. Blooms open in the evening and produce a sweet fragrance that is attractive to hawkmoths. With its long proboscis, this moth probes deeply into the floral tube to feed on nectar. Pollen threads catch on the moth's legs and body as it hovers. When it flits to the next flower, these pollen threads are caught on the sticky stigma, thus effecting pollina-

tion. As the plant dries, the outer leaves curl inward, forming a cage-like structure that gives rise to the alternative common name—bird cage primrose. The large, showy flowers of dune evening primrose are a magnificent sight against the stark beauty of the dune habitats where they are typically found. It often grows in association with sand verbena, an equally handsome wildflower.

Elevation: Below 2,500 feet

Range: Mojave and Sonoran deserts

Spanish Needles
Palafoxia arida

Family
Sunflower–Asteraceae

Spanish needles is a pungent annual that grows to two feet in sandy washes and dune areas. Heads are small clusters of white to lavender, tubular disk flowers. The needlelike achenes, or fruits, explain the origin of the common name. Leaves are narrow, linear, and up to four inches long. A robust variety, *P. arida gigantea,* occurs in western Arizona and can grow to a stunning six feet tall. This extreme height likely is an adaptation for survival in active dune systems where plants can be buried by shifting sands. Spanish needles can be found in bloom as early as February and as late as November, depending on location and conditions. The Cahuilla used this plant in the preparation of a yellow dye.

Elevation: Below 2,000 feet

Range: Mojave and Sonoran deserts

Rock Daisy

Perityle emoryi

Family

Sunflower–Asteraceae

A showy, aromatic, spring annual, rock daisy is often seen nestled in rock crevices on canyon walls. The half-inch flower heads consist of snow-white rays surrounding yellow disk flowers. The distinctive, rich green leaves are slightly succulent, lobed and toothed, and up to four inches long and wide. Rock daisy blooms from February to May and occurs on rocky slopes, and in canyons and sandy washes.

Elevation: 500–8,000 feet

Range: Mojave and Sonoran deserts

Woolly Plantain (Indian Wheat)

Plantago patagonica

Family

Plantain–Plantaginaceae

Woolly plantain is a common and widespread annual that grows only about eight inches high. The tiny, white flowers and papery, translucent petals deserve close inspection with a hand lens. The linear, densely hairy, gray-green leaves arise from the base of the plant to a length of about four inches. Woolly plantain blooms from February to July and occurs on dry slopes or mesas, and especially in sandy and gravelly soils. The fruits contain several seeds per capsule that become sticky when moistened. The Navajo traditionally used woolly plantain as a gastrointestinal aid for adults and colicky babies. The Zuni used the plant to treat diarrhea. The Havasupai and Pima ground the seeds into a mush. A related species of *Plantago* is cultivated in India as an ingredient in a commercial laxative.

Elevation: 1,000–7,000 feet

Range: Canada south to the Mojave, Sonoran, Great Basin, and Chihuahuan deserts

Odora (Poreleaf)
Porophyllum gracile

Family
Sunflower–Asteraceae

Odora would be an easy plant to miss were it not for its pungent aroma. One need only brush against it slightly to release the powerful scent. Look closely on the stems, leaves, and flower heads to see the linear oil glands that are responsible for the smell. Most likely, this is an effective adaptation to deter nibbling by desert animals. The purplish white heads have no rays, only a narrow cluster of disk flowers about three quarters of an inch long. Foliage is dark green, sparse, and threadlike. Odora blooms from March to October and occurs on dry, rocky slopes and mesas, and in washes. The Havasupai used the pounded plant as a liniment for aching muscles, and as a wash for sores. It also was taken internally to relieve abdominal pain. The Seri brewed the stems to make tea that is an effective cold remedy and a child-birth medicine. A tea made from odora roots has been used by the Seri to treat toothache and diarrhea.

Elevation: Below 4,000 feet

Range: Mojave and Sonoran deserts

Desert Chicory
Rafinesquia neomexicana

Family
Sunflower–Asteraceae

Desert chicory is a conspicuous and widespread annual growing to twenty inches tall, with one to few upright stems. Flower heads consist of ray flowers only, white to cream, with finely cut square tips. A faint purple stripe is visible on the underside of the outer rays. This plant is similar to tackstem but has larger rays numbering no more than eighteen, and no tack-like glands. Leaves are mostly basal, pinnately divided, and extend to six inches in length. Desert chicory blooms from February to May in a variety of desert habitats, often under shrubs.

Elevation: 200–3,000 feet

Range: Mojave, Sonoran, and Chihuahuan deserts

Silverbells (Twist Flower)
Streptanthus carinatus (arizonicus)

Family

Mustard–Brassicaceae

Silverbells is an attractive annual or biennial that grows to three and a half feet, with creamy, urn-shaped flowers that appear along erect branches. Blooming from January to April, the flowers are followed by slender, upright pods up to three inches in length. The clasping leaves have basal lobes that reach beyond the stem. A bright yellow variety, *S. carinatus luteus,* can be seen in Organ Pipe Cactus National Monument. Silverbells is common in desert washes or flats, canyons, and open woodlands.

Elevation: 1500–4,500 feet

Range: Sonoran and Chihuahuan deserts

Desert Zinnia
Zinnia acerosa

Family
Sunflower–Asteraceae

Desert zinnia is a showy, somewhat woody perennial that grows to eight inches tall, with stems that branch profusely from the base. One-inch-wide white heads appear intermittently from March to December in response to rain. Ray flowers become papery and dirty white with age. Leaves are needlelike, up to one inch long, and extend the entire length of the stems. The seeds are an excellent food source for quail, finches, and sparrows. Desert zinnia is widespread on rocky slopes and bajadas, and in grasslands.

Elevation: 2,000–5,000 feet

Range: Sonoran and Chihuahuan deserts

Bahia
Bahia absinthifolia

Family
Sunflower–Asteraceae

A perennial with gray-green foliage and showy, yellow flowers, bahia is sometimes confused with desert marigold, though the flower heads are quite different. The rays of Bahia have spaces between them, whereas the flower heads of desert marigold form a solid disk of over-lapping rays. This is most noticeable as you look directly down on the flower. The stems and leaves of Bahia are covered with soft, white hairs. Leaves are toothed or lobed and clustered at the base of the plant. Bahia blooms from April to October and is found on rocky slopes, bajadas, and gravelly flats.

Elevation: 2,500–5,500 feet

Range: Sonoran and Chihuahuan deserts

Desert Marigold
Baileya multiradiata

Family
Sunflower–Asteraceae

A widespread, showy biennial with gray-green foliage and lemon-yellow heads, desert marigold is a pleasant sight along roadsides, slopes, and gravelly flats. It will produce brilliant color with even small amounts of rainfall, and will flower almost year round when moisture is available. Flowers occur on stem tips that rise up to twelve inches above the foliage. Overlapping rays with blunt, finely cut tips form a solid disk around the outer edge of the flower head. Leaves are grayish and covered with woolly hairs. This plant is often sold in nurseries and is easily grown from seed, making it a welcome addition to desert landscapes.

Elevation: Below 5,000 feet

Range: All North American deserts

Yellow Cups (Sundrop)
Camissonia brevipes

Family
Evening Primrose–Onagraceae

Yellow cups is an upright annual with brilliant yellow flowers that grows to a height of up to two feet. Flower buds hang in a pendulous cluster. Individual flowers are one and one half inches wide and have four petals, eight stamens, and a club-like stigma that is characteristic of the genus. Leaves are oval or pinnately lobed, often with a reddish tinge. Yellow cups is common on rocky slopes, in washes, and on gravelly flats. In a good year, yellow cups forms large expanses of color in the landscape.

Elevation: Below 4,500 feet

Range: Mojave and Sonoran deserts

Slim Evening Primrose
Camissonia californica

Family
Evening Primrose–Onagraceae

Slim evening primrose is an annual with single or multiple stems up to three feet tall, and sparse foliage and flowers. The single, pale yellow flowers have small, reddish spots on the petals. Leaves are narrow, linear or lance-shaped, and lobed near the base of the plant. Look for small dark spots on the leaves— a common characteristic of the *Camissonia* genus. The fruit is a slim, upright pod that splits open at maturity, casting out numerous tiny seeds.

Elevation: Below 4,500 feet

Range: Mojave and Sonoran deserts

Brittlebush
Encelia farinosa

Family
Sunflower–Asteraceae

A bundant on dry slopes, this showy perennial will tint the hillsides with yellow color if winter rains are plentiful. Brittlebush is a common desert shrub two to three feet tall and wide with silvery, gray-green foliage. A bouquet of bright yellow, daisy-like flower heads reaches high above the plant itself, giving the appearance of a mass of gold. Sometimes called *incienso*, brittlebush stems contain a resin used for incense in Mexican churches. The Tohono O'odham used

the resin as a chewing gum and as glue to fasten arrow points to shafts. Similarly, the Seri used this resin as glue for fastening harpoon tips, treating sores, and sealing pottery. The Cahuilla used the leaves, stems, and blossoms to treat toothaches. Today, brittlebush is a popular landscape plant in many parts of the desert southwest.

Elevation: Below 3,000 feet

Range: Mojave, Sonoran, and Great Basin deserts

Desert Trumpet
Eriogonum inflatum

Family
Buckwheat–Polygonaceae

Desert trumpet is an annual or biennial buckwheat with a large inflated stem that rises up to three feet from a basal rosette of round or heart-shaped leaves. The swollen stem is thought to be caused from irritation by a moth larva that lives inside. Flowers are pale yellow to reddish, and form tiny clusters on branch tips. The remarkable stems have a graceful, tapered look and are sometimes used in dried arrangements. The Havasupai once cooked the leaves as a vegetable and pounded the seeds to make porridge. The Yavapai sometimes used the inflated stems as a smoking pipe for tobacco.

Elevation: Below 3,000 feet

Range: Great Basin, Mojave, and Sonoran deserts

Desert Sunflower

Geraea canescens

Family
Sunflower–Asteraceae

Desert sunflower is a striking annual that grows up to three feet in height if conditions are favorable. Flower heads are brilliant yellow, about two inches wide, and occur on the stem tips. The toothed leaves are oval to lance-shaped, with prominent veins and long, stiff hairs that make them rough to the touch. The fragrant flowers bloom from January to June and are attractive to moths, bees, and many other insects. This species can be extremely abundant on sandy soils in a good year, creating spectacular rivers of gold color across miles of gravelly flats and sandy valleys. The plentiful seeds provide an important food source for birds and rodents.

Elevation: Below 3,000 feet

Range: Mojave and Sonoran deserts

Telegraph Plant (Camphorweed)

Heterotheca subaxillaris

Family
Sunflower–Asteraceae

A conspicuous roadside annual in spring and summer, telegraph plant can grow to a height of two to six feet under moist conditions. The plant has sticky stems and leaves and bright yellow flowers on branch tips. Crushed leaves have a strong medicinal smell. Although it can be toxic when taken internally, telegraph plant is considered a useful medicinal plant in parts of Mexico, where the flowers are used in a preparation to treat inflammations. Leaves also are used as an antiseptic for wounds, and to relieve swelling in rheumatic joints.

Elevation: 1,000–5,500 feet

Range: Sonoran and Chihuahuan deserts, and widespread in the eastern, southern, and midwestern U.S.

Coulter's Hibiscus (Rose Mallow)
Hibiscus coulteri

Family
Mallow–Malvaceae

Rose mallow is an erect perennial with sparse foliage and spindly stems that can reach up to four feet in height. It often is found growing up through shrubs. The large, lovely, two-inch-wide flowers resemble a pale yellow rose as they begin to open. Peering into the flower, you'll notice a red spot at the base of each petal and an ornate, reddish stigma divided into five velvety pads. Stamens are united on a single column, typical of the mallow family. Upper leaves are three-lobed, with faint reddish margins and fine hairs. Fruits split open at maturity and release several hairy seeds. The unique, star-shaped capsule remnant persists on the plant long after the seeds have fallen. Rose mallow blooms intermittently from February to November in response to rain.

Elevation: 1,500–4,000 feet

Range: Sonoran and Chihuahuan deserts

Janusia
Janusia gracilis

Family
Malpighia–Malpighiaceae

Janusia is a common desert vine or shrub with small, but attractive, yellow flowers. The slender stems will twine up to nine feet in length over cacti, trees, and shrubs. Flowers are a half inch wide with fringed petals that narrow at the base. Leaves are narrow and linear. Oil-gathering bees pollinate the flowers, reaching between the petals for the oil glands on the underside of the sepals. Janusia will bloom inter-mittently from April to October. The unusual, pale coral fruits are winged, like a maple, and dry to a blond color.

Elevation: 1,000–5,000 feet

Range: Sonoran and Chihuahuan deserts

Bladder Pod

Lesquerella gordonii

Family
Mustard–Brassicaceae

B ladder pod is an early spring annual that forms carpets of yellow color with abundant fall and winter rain. Flowers have four petals and six stamens, typical of the mustard family. Leaves are linear or lobed and up to two inches long. After pollination, fruits develop into spherical, pea-sized, inflated pods. Bladder pod occurs on flats, slopes, and bajadas and blooms from January to April.

Elevation: 100–5,000 feet

Range: Sonoran and Chihuahuan deserts

Spiny Goldenweed
Machaeranthera pinnatifida

Family
Sunflower–Asteraceae

B ranching from a somewhat woody base, the stems of spiny
goldenweed grow to a height of anywhere from eight to twenty
inches. The flower heads are a typical yellow daisy type, about an
inch wide with narrow ray flowers. Leaves are pinnately divided
or toothed and lobed, all with bristly tips. This is a highly variable
species and may not appear quite the same in different localities.

Elevation: 2,100–6,000 feet

Range: Mojave, Sonoran, and Chihuahuan deserts

Desert Dandelion
Malacothrix californica var. glabrata

Family
Sunflower–Asteraceae

A common spring annual up to eighteen inches tall, desert dandelion has showy pale yellow flower heads and produces vast patches of color in a good year. The heads consist solely of ray flowers, with the center ones forming a dot of red color. Often a single plant will have numerous heads in bloom. Desert dandelion is found on rocky slopes and bajadas and sandy desert flats, blooming from spring to early summer.

Elevation: Below 7,000 feet

Range: Mojave, Sonoran, and Great Basin deserts

Menodora (Twinberry)
Menodora scabra

Family
Olive–Oleaceae

M enodora is a shrubby perennial growing to two and a half feet tall, with clear yellow, three-quarter-inch-wide flowers. Sparse, linear leaves hug the stems; leaves and stems are covered with rough, scabrous hairs. The unique, spherical, paired capsules are translucent. As the capsule dries, the cap falls away, releasing two or three curved, textured seeds. Menodora occurs on rocky slopes and bajadas, blooming from April to November. The Navajo used the root to treat back pain and heartburn, and to facilitate labor.

Elevation: 1,500–7,500 feet

Range: Mojave, Sonoran, and Chihuahuan deserts

Blazing Star
Mentzelia jonesii (nitens)

Family
Stickleaf–Loasaceae

B lazing star is an annual growing up to two feet tall, with bright
yellow flowers in small clusters on branch tips. Petals are
shiny and iridescent. The fruit is a one-seeded, club-shaped capsule
with sepals attached to the tip. Stems, foliage, and seed pods of
blazing star are covered with stiff, barbed hairs that can stick to
clothing, shoes, and the fur of
passing animals. This adaptation
helps to disperse the seed far
from the mother plant where
conditions might be more favorable for germination. There are
many annual species similar to
blazing star.

Elevation: Below 3,000 feet

Range: Great Basin, Mojave,
and Sonoran deserts

Stickleaf Mentzelia

Mentzelia multiflora (pumila)

Family
Stickleaf–Loasaceae

Opening late in the day, the flowers of stickleaf mentzelia are showy, bright yellow, and up to two inches across. The plant blooms from spring through fall. The long, narrow leaves have a coarse texture; stems are whitish and up to three feet tall. This plant can be found in a broad range of elevations and a variety of habitats, ranging from desert to pine forest.

Elevation: Below 8,000 feet

Range: Great Basin and Sonoran deserts

Silverpuffs
Microseris linearifolia

Family
Sunflower–Asteraceae

A widespread annual, silverpuffs grows to about one foot in height. The flower resembles a dandelion, with the exception of the long, pointed bracts, which extend beyond the one-inch-wide head. The striking, silvery seed head forms an unusual geometric shape, delicately held together until the wind shatters the symmetry and successfully spreads the seeds. Silverpuffs blooms from March to April and is found on rocky slopes, roadsides, and disturbed areas. Leaves are basal and pinnately lobed. Flowering stems are hollow.

Elevation: Below 5,000 feet

Range: Great Basin, Sonoran, and Chihuahuan deserts

Spring Evening Primrose
Oenothera primiveris

Family
Evening Primrose–Onagraceae

The lovely, pale yellow flowers of spring evening primrose open at dusk to form a two-inch-wide blossom. Hawkmoths are likely the primary pollinator for this plant because their long proboscis is uniquely adapted to reach deep into the floral tube to probe for nectar. As they do so, the sticky pollen clings to their bodies and is transferred to other plants. Spring evening primrose is found on rocky slopes and gravelly bajadas, washes, and arroyos, and blooms from February to April.

Elevation: Below 4,000 feet

Range: All North American deserts

Desert Velvet (Turtle-back)
Psathyrotes ramossisima

Family
Sunflower–Asteraceae

Desert velvet is a perennial that forms a distinctive, compact, dome-shaped mound up to a foot across. It is this shape that gave rise to the alternative common name: turtle-back. The entire plant is covered with soft, velvety, white hairs, which give it a silvery appearance. Tiny, golden flower heads are almost hidden among the foliage. The coarsely toothed leaves have prominent, sunken veins and smell like turpentine when crushed.

Elevation: Below 1,500 feet

Range: Mojave and Sonoran deserts

Paperflower

Psilostrophe cooperi

Family
Sunflower–Asteraceae

A common perennial shrub with yellow flowers and bluish gray foliage, paperflower typically stands about one to two feet in height. The profusion of showy, one-inch flower heads makes this plant a standout in the desert landscape. The rays become papery as they age, fading to blond. Leaves are linear and up to three inches long. Paperflower blooms almost year round depending on local conditions, and is common on sandy plains and in washes. The Apache and Zuni used the blossoms for a yellow dye.

Elevation: 2,100–4,300 feet

Range: Mojave and Sonoran deserts

Desert Senna
Senna covesii

Family
Legume–Fabaceae

A widespread perennial in the legume family, desert senna has showy, one-inch, mustard-yellow flowers, and pinnate leaves on plants up to a foot tall. Desert senna is pollinated by carpenter bees and bumblebees, which vibrate their wing muscles as they hang upside down on the flower. This causes the pollen to shake out of the anther pore and cover the body of the bee. Sleepy orange and cloudless sulphur butterflies use desert senna as a larval food plant. The pods dry to a dusty, chocolate brown, split partially to release the seeds, and remain on the plant for many weeks or months. The Seri made a tea of the root to treat measles, chicken pox, and kidney and liver problems.

Elevation: 1,000–3,000 feet

Range: Mojave, Sonoran, and Chihuahuan deserts

Dogweed (Parralena)
Thymophylla (Dyssodia) pentachaeta

Family
Sunflower–Asteraceae

Dogweed is a low-growing perennial with delicate, aromatic foliage and bright, golden-yellow flower heads. Branching from the base and growing only four to eight inches high, dogweed bears flower heads about two thirds of an inch wide, and will bloom intermittently from spring through late fall. Dogweed provides both nectar and larval food for the dainty sulphur, a tiny, pale yellow butterfly. Dogweed often is used in desert gardens as a sun-loving groundcover.

Elevation: 2,500–4,500 feet

Range: Mojave, Sonoran, and Chihuahuan deserts

Fiddleneck
Amsinckia intermedia

Family
Borage–Boraginaceae

A common annual that grows to a height of two feet, fiddleneck will bloom from March through May. The small, tubular blossoms are a vibrant golden orange and are borne on numerous, coiled spikes. The entire plant is covered with stiff, white, bristly hairs. Fiddleneck is common in disturbed sites, as well as slopes, bajadas, flats, and washes. The plant contains alkaloids that make it poisonous to livestock. The leaves, however, were once boiled and eaten by the Pima.

Elevation: Below 4,000 feet

Range: Sonoran Desert

Desert Honeysuckle
Anisacanthus thurberi

Family

Acanthus–Acanthaceae

O ccuring primarily in desert washes, desert honeysuckle is a perennial shrub with erect stems and shredded white bark that grows five to six feet tall. Foliage is sparse and often non-existent during extended dry or cold periods. The burnt-orange to reddish flowers are one to one-and-one-half inches long, tubular, and attractive to hummingbirds. Blooms appear along the stems primarily in spring, but also can occur in fall, or whenever conditions are favorable. The fruit is a flattened capsule that contains two large seeds. The Acanthus family is mainly tropical; only a few species occur in North American deserts.

Elevation: 2,500–5,500 feet

Range: Sonoran Desert

Mariposa Lily
Calochortus kennedyi

Family
Lily–Liliaceae

M ariposa lily is a large and lovely flower, especially when viewed closely from above. Three broad, deep-orange petals each bear a fringed, purplish spot at the base. The three-parted stigma is large and visible. A few narrow, grassy leaves emerge from an underground bulb in fall or winter. In late spring, one to several flowers bloom. Seen at a distance, the rich orange flowers are sometimes mistaken for poppies. Although usually scattered and uncommon, in a good year masses of mariposa lilies can be seen on rocky hillsides. The bulbs of various species of mariposa lily have been eaten, roasted or raw, by many tribes throughout the West.

Elevation: Below 5,000 feet

Range: Mojave and Sonoran deserts

Mexican Goldpoppy
Eschscholtzia mexicana

Family
Poppy–Papaveraceae

Surely one of the most spectacular desert annuals, the Mexican goldpoppy forms dazzling carpets of gold in a good wildflower year. Large, showy flowers have a shiny, iridescent texture, with the base of each petal often tinted with orange. Tiny blister beetles pollinate these flowers, which ultimately give way to long, spiky fruits that split when mature and cast out numerous, small black seeds. Many desert gardeners sow goldpoppy seed in the fall to produce their own showy springtime display. The similar California poppy (*Eschscholtzia californica*) is larger in size and orange in color.

Elevation: Below 4,500 feet

Range: Mojave, Sonoran, and Chihuahuan deserts

Herissantia
Herissantia crispa

Family
Mallow–Malvaceae

Herissantia is a weak-stemmed, shrubby perennial bearing three-quarter-inch-wide, pale gold flowers. The unmistakable fruits look like hairy, ribbed, and flattened spheres. Typical of many mallows, the leaves are heart-shaped, toothed, gray-green, and hairy. Herissantia blooms almost year round and occurs on rocky slopes and in canyons.

Elevation: Below 3,500 feet

Range: Sonoran and Chihuahuan deserts and tropical America

Summer Poppy (Arizona Poppy)
Kallstroemia grandiflora

Family
Caltrop–Zygophyllaceae

Summer poppy is a showy summer annual with a prostrate habit and pinnate leaves. The one- to one-and-one-half-inch, richly colored apricot flowers superficially resemble poppies. In fact, summer

poppy is a member of the caltrop family and is thus related to creosote bush, and to an invasive weed known as goat head or puncture vine. Summer poppy is most common in grasslands but does occur sporadically in desert habitats. It blooms from July to October.

Elevation: Below 5,000 feet

Range: Sonoran and Chihuahuan deserts

Desert Globemallow

Sphaeralcea ambigua

Family
Mallow–Malvaceae

Desert globemallow is a common, short-lived perennial with attractive, three-quarter-inch, cup-shaped flowers that are usually bright orange. Other color forms include red, pink, purple, and white. The plants flower heavily in spring and intermittently throughout the summer. Also known as sore eye poppy, hairs on the leaves of this plant can irritate the eyes if accidental contact occurs. The Seri used the bark of the root to make a tea for the treatment for diarrhea and sore throat. The Hopi used the root of a related species to combat diarrhea.

Elevation: Below 3,500 feet

Range: Mojave and Sonoran deserts

Desert Paintbrush (Painted Cup)

Castilleja chromosa

Family

Figwort–Scrophulariaceae

Desert paintbrush is a perennial with multiple stems that grows up to eighteen inches tall. The actual flowers are greenish, inconspicuous, and somewhat hidden within the showy clusters of reddish orange bracts. The lower leaves are linear to lance-shaped. Desert paintbrush blooms March to September and occurs in a broad range of elevations, from deserts to pine forests. The Hopi used a related species extensively in ceremonies, and as a medicine to ease menstrual pain.

Elevation:
2,000–8,000 feet

Range: Mojave, Sonoran, and Great Basin deserts

Chuparosa
Justicia californica

Family
Acanthus–Acanthaceae

An extremely drought-hardy shrub that will bloom almost year round, chuparosa can grow to a height of up to six feet. The common name is a Spanish word for hummingbird, and indeed the tubular, red-orange flowers attract them effectively. In some parts of the Sonoran Desert, migrating hummingbirds depend on chuparosa nectar for sustenance along their route. Chuparosa is a popular landscape plant in desert gardens.

Elevation:
200–2,500 feet

Range: Sonoran Desert

Brownfoot
Acourtia (Perezia) wrightii

Family
Sunflower–Asteraceae

Growing up to two feet in height, brownfoot is a perennial with clusters of tiny, fragrant, lavender-pink flowers. The leaves are distinctively wavy-edged, with prominent, spiny teeth. Blooming from March to May, brownfoot attracts numerous butterflies and bees. It is often found under trees and shrubs in canyons, on hillsides, and in desert grasslands. A related species—*A. nana,* known as desert holly—grows only about five inches tall, smells like violets, and typically is found in drier habitats.

Brownfoot leaves have been used in a poultice by the Hualapai to treat wounds. The Navajo used brownfoot leaves as a post-partum medicine.

Elevation: Below 6,000 feet

Range: Sonoran, Great Basin, and Chihuahuan deserts

Freckled Milkvetch (Locoweed)

Astragalus lentiginosus

Family

Legume–Fabaceae

Freckled milkvetch is a perennial that grows up to two feet tall, with handsome reddish purple flowers that bloom from February to May. The pinnate leaves, "pea" flowers, and characteristic inflated pods make this plant easy to identify as a type of locoweed. This species has a spotted or "freckled" pod, with a long, pointed beak. A.*lentiginosus* is extremely widespread and variable, with more than thirty-eight recognized varieties. Some locoweeds have been known to cause poisoning in livestock.

Elevation: 300–12,000 feet

Range: All North American deserts to northwest U.S.

Owl Clover (Escobita)
Castilleja exserta (Orthocarpus purpurascens)

Family
Figwort–Scrophulariaceae

Growing four to fifteen inches tall, owl clover is a small but brilliantly colored spring annual that forms carpets of rose-purple blooms in years with abundant rainfall. The half-inch flowers are nestled within the brightly colored floral bracts and are tipped with yellow or white. The flowers and bracts are densely clustered around the stem tips. "Escobita" means "little broom" in Spanish. Occurring in gravelly desert flats and desert grasslands, owl clover blooms from March to May.

Elevation: 1,500–4,500 feet

Range: Mojave, Sonoran, and Great Basin deserts

Larkspur (Barestem Larkspur)

Delphinium scaposum

Family

Crowfoot–Ranunculaceae

The handsome, asymmetrical, deep royal blue to purple flowers of larkspur are borne along flowering stems that ascend to three feet in height. These stems emerge from a basal rosette of highly divided leaves. The flowers have five large sepals and five smaller ones, with the upper sepal forming a long spur that contains nectar. Bumblebees pollinate larkspur by "burrowing" into the flowers to reach the nectar-rich spur. The plants contain poisonous alkaloids that deter nibbling by desert animals. Larkspur

occurs on dry slopes and in canyons and desert washes, and flowers from February to April. The Navajo and Hopi have used larkspur petals, seeds, and pollen in ceremonies.

Elevation: Below 5,000 feet

Range: Mojave, Sonoran, and Chihuahuan deserts

Blue Dicks (Desert Hyacinth)

Dichelostemma pulchellum

Family

Lily–Liliaceae

B lue dicks is a perennial lily that blooms in early spring with clusters of lavender-purple flowers on slender stems up to two feet tall. Look for the prominent purple midvein on each petal. The thin, grassy leaves begin to wither as the flowers bloom. Blue dicks is a very common species on dry, rocky slopes in deserts and in grasslands. The bulbs were once dug and eaten raw or cooked by many tribes, including the Tohono O'odham, Pima, Apache, and Cahuilla.

Elevation: Below 6,000 feet

Range: Present in all North American deserts

Filaree (Crane's Bill, Heron's Bill)
Erodium cicutarium

Family
Geranium–Geraniaceae

Filaree, though attractive, is a highly invasive weed. Native to Europe, it is now widely naturalized throughout North America. The fern-like foliage grows in a prostrate rosette. Small, pinkish-lavender flowers arise in small clusters on stalks up to fifteen inches tall. These become the odd, needlelike, spiky fruits that resemble a crane's bill. These fruits are examples of a unique adaptation. As the fruits dry, they curl into "corkscrews." When moisture arrives, they uncurl and actually drive the seeds into the soil, thus facilitating the chances of successful germination.

Elevation: Below 7,000 feet

Range: Found in a variety of habitats throughout North America

Stork's Bill

Erodium texanum

Family
Geranium–Geraniaceae

The magenta flowers of stork's bill have petals up to one inch long and bloom in small clusters late in the day. Leaves are up to two inches long with rounded lobes. As the beak-like pods dry, they coil in much the same way as the pods of filaree. Stork's bill blooms from February to April and is common on gravelly flats, along washes, and in desert grass-lands. Unlike filaree, stork's bill is a native, non-invasive species.

Elevation: 1,000–4,500 feet

Range: Great Basin, Sonoran, and Chihuahuan deserts

Arizona Blue Eyes

Evolvulus alsinoides

Family
Morning Glory–Convolvulaceae

A diminutive perennial with half-inch, sky blue, circular blooms, Arizona blue eyes is a lovely sight on canyon trails from spring to fall. Flowers occur on slender stalks along the spreading, semi-prostrate stems. Leaves are gray-green, hairy, and lance-shaped. Arizona blue eyes is found on rocky slopes, along washes, and in grasslands.

Elevation: 2,200–5,000 feet

Range: Sonoran and Chihuahuan deserts and south to South America

Goodding Verbena (Desert Verbena)
Glandularia (verbena) gooddingii

Family

Verbena–Verbenaceae

Goodding verbena forms an attractive, low mound with multiple stems that bear clusters of small, lavender blossoms. Verbenas are short-lived perennials that are a common sight along desert washes and on rocky slopes. Flowers open in the evening and emit a sweet fragrance that attracts hawkmoths. In the daytime, several types of butterflies also will visit the flowers. Goodding verbena will bloom almost year round, depending on conditions, and is commonly cultivated as a colorful groundcover in desert gardens.

Elevation: Below 5,000 feet

Range: All North American deserts

Rock Hibiscus
Hibiscus denudatus

Family
Mallow–Malvaceae

R ock hibiscus is a perennial growing to one and a half feet tall, with several straggly stems arising from the base of the plant. The exquisite, lavender, one-and-one-half-inch flowers are showy, with petals that turn deep pink toward the center of the flower. Elliptical, densely hairy, gray-green leaves are sparse to nonexistent on the plant, depending on conditions. A five-chambered seed capsule forms and splits at maturity to release several large, hairy seeds. The star-shaped capsule remnant remains on the plant for many weeks or months. Rock hibiscus is found on dry slopes and in desert washes and blooms intermittently from January to October.

Elevation: Below 4,500 feet

Range: Sonoran and Chihuahuan deserts

Range Ratany

Krameria erecta

Family
Krameria–Krameriaceae

A freely branching, gray-stemmed shrub with small, linear leaves, range ratany grows two to three feet tall and is covered with handsome, three-quarter-inch, magenta flowers in spring. It's helpful to look closely at the unique structure of these highly asymmetrical flowers. The brightly colored sepals are large and easily mistaken for petals. The actual petals are smaller, with three upper, stalked petals and two lower, fleshy ones. The flowers produce an oil rather than nectar to reward bees that serve as pollinators. Bees collect the oil, mix it with pollen, and bring the mixture to their nests as larval food. Range ratany pro-

duces odd, globular fruits with hooked spines that often are infested by moth larvae. The plant is a partial parasite, obtaining nutrients through the roots of nearby shrubs. Range ratany blooms from April to November and occurs on rocky slopes, gravelly bajadas, and in desert grasslands. The Seri used the bark of the roots of white ratany (*K. grayi*) to make a dye for baskets. The Pima used the powdered roots to treat sores.

Elevation: Below 5,000 feet

Range: Mojave, Sonoran, and Chihuahuan deserts

Blue Flax
Linum lewisii

Family
Linum–Linaceae

Extremely widespread and commonly cultivated, blue flax is an attractive perennial with two-inch-wide, sky-blue flowers. The shiny petals usually wilt and drop by noon. Leaves are narrow and threadlike and ascend the entire length of the unbranched stems. Blue flax blooms from spring to fall and is found in a wide range of habitats. Broadly distributed, blue flax was used by many tribes in different ways. The Navajo used blue flax to treat headaches and heartburn. Northern tribes ate the seeds and used the strong, fibrous stems to make string, cordage, baskets, fishing nets, and mesh for snowshoes.

Elevation: Below 9,000 feet

Range: All North American deserts and various habitats in western U.S.

Arizona Lupine

Lupinus arizonicus

Family
Legume–Fabaceae

Arizona lupine is a stunning annual with two-foot-high stalks of dark pink to lavender-purple, pea-like flowers. The flowers have a yellow spot on the banner petal that serves as a nectar guide for bees. After pollination, this spot turns reddish purple, which discourages other bees from visiting these flowers. The palmately compound leaves actually "track" the movement of the sun throughout the day. Arizona lupine blooms from January to May and is typically found along roadsides and in desert washes. Many species of lupine occur in a wide range of habitats. The Big Bend Bluebonnet of Texas (*Lupinus havardii*) grows to three feet tall and forms vast fields in a good year. To successfully germinate lupine in a garden, pour boiling water over the seeds and soak them overnight before sowing.

Elevation: Below 4,500 feet

Range: Mojave and Sonoran deserts

Desert Lupine
Lupinus sparsiflorus

Family
Legume–Fabaceae

Common on rocky slopes, roadsides, and washes, desert lupine is a spring annual that grows to about one and a half feet high. Flowers are violet-blue, with a yellow spot on the banner petal. The fruit is a few-seeded, hairy, upright pod. In a good year, desert lupine often is seen growing with Mexican goldpoppy in vast carpets of color. Desert lupine is extremely widespread and prefers sandy soils.

Elevation: Below 3,000 feet

Range: Mojave and Sonoran deserts

Broom Rape
Orobanche ludoviciana *var.* cooperi

Family
Broom Rape–Orobanchaceae

A fleshy-stemmed, parasitic plant that lacks chlorophyll, broomrape has purplish brown stems and flowers on a spike that can be as high as fifteen inches. Parasitic on bursage and other shrubs, broomrape occurs in a wide range of habitats. Broom rape was eaten, cooked or raw, by the Pima and Tohono O'odham.

Elevation: Below 7,000 feet

Range: Great Basin, Sonoran, and Chihuahuan deserts

Sand Bells
Nama hispidum

Family
Water Leaf–Hydrophyllaceae

Occurring primarily in sandy soils, sand bells has delicate, half-inch, lavender flowers on branching stems that reach only about five inches high. Blossoms are tubular with spreading lobes and a pale yellow throat. Depending on soil moisture, sand bells may consist of few flowers or grow into a large, low mound. In a good year, sand bells can be extremely abundant, forming carpets in desert flats and blooming throughout the spring.

Elevation: Below 5,000 feet

Range: Great Basin and Sonoran deserts

Desert Bluebells
(Desert Canterbury Bells)
Phacelia campanularia

Family
Water Leaf–Hydrophyllaceae

Desert Bluebells is an unusually handsome spring annual with large, bell-shaped blossoms and lush, rounded leaves. Flowers are a rich, deep blue, an inch or more long and wide, with flared, rounded petal lobes. The leaves are dark green, with scalloped edges that are tinged with red. Desert bluebells is found on gravelly plains and along washes and blooms from February to April. It can be germinated easily from seed in fall to produce a showy spring display.

Elevation: Below 4,000 feet

Range: Mojave and Sonoran deserts

Scorpionweed (Wild Heliotrope)
Phacelia distans

Family
Water Leaf–Hydrophyllaceae

Scorpionweed is a common spring annual with reddish, branching stems that grow up to thirty inches high in favorable conditions. The small, pale blue to purple blossoms are borne on coiled spikes that are reminiscent of a scorpion's tail. Foliage is pinnately divided and finely haired. Scorpionweed blooms from February to May and typically grows under trees and shrubs along washes and on rocky slopes. Many species of scorpionweed thrive in Southwest deserts. The leaves of Scorpionweed were boiled and eaten by the Pima.

Elevation: 1,000–4,700 feet

Range: Mojave and Sonoran deserts

Chia

Salvia columbariae

Family
Mint–Labiatae

A member of the mint family, chia is an annual with tubular, lavender-purple flowers arranged in dense clusters on square, erect stems. The unique, textured leaves have a minty fragrance and are clustered at the base of the stems. The Pima and Tohono O'odham make a refreshing beverage by steeping the seeds in water. The seeds also have been eaten raw and parched. Chia is found along sandy washes and on dry slopes.

Elevation: Below 3,000 feet

Range: Mojave and Sonoran deserts

Silverleaf Nightshade
(Horse Nettle)
Solanum eleagnifolium

Family
Nightshade–Solanaceae

The attractive, lavender to dark purple, one-inch flowers of silverleaf nightshade crown the branch tips in loose clusters. The light gray elliptical leaves have wavy margins and sharp spines on the undersides. Fruits are round, yellow berries that eventually turn very dark. Growing to a height of about two feet, silverleaf nightshade is common along roadsides and in other disturbed areas. Though attractive, it is considered a highly invasive weed. The plant was introduced from the Plains states and has been spreading rapidly throughout the West.

Elevation: 1,000–5,000 feet

Range: All North American deserts, Kansas and Colorado, and south to South America

GLOSSARY

Achene–a small, hard, one-seeded fruit that does not split open

Alkaloid–a toxic substance produced in a plant that sometimes has medicinal properties

Annual–a plant that completes its life cycle in one year

Anthers–the enlarged, pollen-containing parts of a stamen

Banner–upper petal of a legume flower

Basal–at the base of the plant

Biennial–a plant that completes its life cycle in two years

Bract–a modified leaf, often at the base of a flower or flower cluster

Bulb–a thick, fleshy stem that forms below ground and functions in food storage

Calyx–collective term for the sepals of a flower, usually green

Capsule–a dry fruit with one or more compartments that splits longitudinally or around the circumference

Corolla–a collective term for the petals of a flower

Disk flower–the small, tubular flowers present in the central part of a floral head, as in most members of the sunflower family

Fruit–the ripened ovary with its seed(s)

Gland–a small structure that usually secretes oil or nectar

Parasite–a plant that grows on and derives nourishment from another living plant

Pendulous–hanging or drooping

Perennial–a plant with a life cycle of more that two years

Petal–a basic unit of the corolla that usually is brightly colored

Pinnate leaf–one of a series of leaflets arranged in two rows along a common axis

Pollen–spores formed in the anthers that produce the male cells

Pollination–the transfer of pollen from an anther to a stigma

Prostrate–flat on the ground

Ray flower–a strap-like corolla that is present in many floral heads of the sunflower family

Sepal–one of the segments of the outer whorl of flower parts, usually green

Stamens–the male part of the flower consisting of the filament and anther

Stigma–the pollen-receptive part of a pistil

INDEX

ADDITIONAL READING

Arizona Sonora Desert Museum. *A Natural History of the Sonoran Desert*. Tucson: Arizona-Sonora Desert Museum Press, 2000.

Bowers, Janice Emily. *Flowers and Shrubs of the Mojave Desert*. Tucson: Southwest Parks and Monument Association, 1998.

Dodge, Natt N. *Flowers of the Southwest Deserts*. Tucson: Southwest Parks and Monuments Association, 1985.

Epple, Anne. *A Field Guide to the Plants of Arizona*. Helena, MT: Falcon Publishing, Inc. 1995.

Felger, Richard and Mary Beck Moser. *People of the Desert and Sea: Ethnobotany of the Seri*. Tucson: University of Arizona Press, 1985.

Moerman, Daniel. *Native American Ethnobotany*. Portland, OR: Timber Press, 1998.

Niehaus, Theodore F. et. al. *A Field Guide to Southwestern and Texas Wildflowers*. New York: Houghton Mifflin, 1984.

Taylor, Ronald J. *Desert Wildflowers of North America*. Missoula, MT: Mountain Press Publishing Company, 1998.